Original Title: 101 Strange But True Billiards
Facts.

Authors: Víctor Martínez Cerdá and Carlos
Martínez Cerdá (V&C Brothers)

Layout and design: V&C Brothers

101

STRANGE BUT TRUE

BILLIARDS FACTS

INCREDIBLE AND SURPRISING EVENTS

1

The history of billiard balls is fascinating and has a long evolution throughout the centuries.

In their beginnings, billiard balls were made of a variety of materials such as wood, clay, and stone.

However, as the game became more popular, players began to demand higher quality balls that were more consistent in their weight and smoothness.

It was then when ivory began to be used to make billiard balls, as it was a strong and durable material.

However, the manufacture of ivory billiard balls was an extremely expensive and laborious process, as an entire elephant tusk was needed to make just three or four balls.

Furthermore, elephant hunting for ivory became a major problem for the conservation of the species.

Fortunately, in the 1860s, the Hyatt brothers discovered nitrocellulose, a material that proved to be an excellent alternative to ivory.

Nitrocellulose was easier to work with than ivory and allowed for mass production of billiard balls.

In addition, nitrocellulose balls were more resistant to impacts and less prone to chipping or wearing than ivory balls.

Later, in the 1920s, chemist Leo Baekeland invented Bakelite, a phenolic resin that became the standard material for billiard ball production.

Bakelite was even more resistant and durable than nitrocellulose, and allowed for mass production of high-quality billiard balls.

Since then, most billiard balls have been made with Bakelite or similar materials.

2

American pool is the only billiards variant that is played with numbered balls, while other variants such as snooker and blackball use balls of different colors to differentiate them.

The reason behind this difference in ball numbering is not clear, as there is no definitive explanation that justifies the decision.

It is believed that numbering the balls in American pool may have arisen from the need to follow the correct sequence of balls during the game.

In American pool, the objective is to hit the balls in numerical order, starting with ball number 1 and ending with ball number 9 (or 10 in the game known as "ten-ball").

Numbering the balls may have been a way to help players remember which ball they should hit next.

However, in other billiards variants such as snooker, the sequence of balls is not as important as in American pool.

In snooker, for example, the goal is to hit the colored balls in the correct order, but not necessarily in a specific numerical sequence.

Therefore, there is no need to number the balls in snooker or other similar variants.

3

**The use of chalk in billiards began
in the mid-19th century.**

It is believed that the use of chalk for striking the ball
was discovered by an English teacher named Jack Carr.

Carr discovered that by applying a small amount of chalk
to the tip of the billiard cue before striking the ball,
a greater grip between the cue tip and the ball could
be achieved, allowing for a spin effect on the ball.

This effect is known as "English" in honor of Carr.

The use of chalk in billiards has become a
common practice among billiard players.

Chalk is used to keep the billiard cue tip in
optimal condition for striking the ball.

Chalk helps to absorb moisture and grease that can
accumulate on the cue tip, which can affect the
quality of the shot and the accuracy of the strike.

In addition, chalk can also help reduce the friction
between the cue tip and the ball,
making it easier to strike.

4

In American pool, the official white ball for competitions has the same measurements and weight as the rest of the balls.

However, in some leisure venues and recreational rooms, the white ball may be slightly larger to differentiate it from the rest of the balls when it falls into the pockets.

This is done to facilitate the identification of the white ball at the bottom of the pockets and to help players avoid mistakes in choosing the appropriate ball for the next shot.

In the case of English billiards, the white ball is smaller than the rest of the balls.

The white ball in English billiards usually has a diameter of 44.5 mm, while the diameter of the other balls is usually 52.5 mm.

This difference in the size of the white ball is due to the differences in the way different types of billiards are played.

In English billiards, the goal is to hit a specific ball and send it to a specific pocket.

The white ball is used to strike the other balls and position them for the next shot.

Because the white ball is not used directly to score points in English billiards, it has been made smaller to avoid obstructing the view of the target ball.

5

In American pool, the colors of balls 4 and 12 were changed from purple to pink to make them more visible on television screens.

Purple, as a dark color, didn't show up well in televised broadcasts, so it was decided to switch to a brighter and more easily visible color.

Pink is a color that shows up clearly on television and stands out against the green background of the pool table.

In some American pool games, the color cyan is also used for ball 7 instead of brown.

This is done to avoid visual confusion between brown balls and green balls on the pool table.

Brown and green balls can be difficult to distinguish under certain lighting conditions and for some players, especially those with visual impairments.

It's important to note that these modifications to ball colors are not universal in all American pool games.

Local or casual games may often use different combinations of ball colors, and some players may have their own personal preferences.

However, in official American pool competitions, rules established by the Billiard and Carom Association of the United States (BCA) are followed, which specify the official ball colors.

6

**The history of billiards is somewhat uncertain,
and there are different theories about its origins.**

Some historians suggest that similar games to billiards were played in
ancient Egypt and Persia, but modern billiards as we know it today
appears to have originated in Europe in the 15th century.

It's believed that the game of billiards evolved from other games
with sticks and balls that were played in medieval Europe.

The first billiards games were played outdoors with wooden sticks
and balls, and the aim was to hit a ball through an
arch or to touch a post or stake.

In the 15th century, billiards moved indoors and began
to be played on tables covered with green felt.

The balls were made of ivory and the cues were made of wood.

By the 17th century, billiards had become very popular throughout
Europe, and the manufacturing of billiard tables and
ivory balls became a significant industry.

As for the theory that billiards was invented by the French,
there is some evidence suggesting that the game
may have originated in France.

In medieval France, a similar game to billiards called "Jeu de mail"
was played with a ball and mallet on an outdoor field.

In any case, billiards has evolved over the centuries
and has become a popular sport worldwide.

Today, there are many variations of the game,
each with its own rules and traditions.

7

**Billiards was the first sport to have
a world championship.**

This historic event took place in 1873 in the
city of London, England, where the first
World Billiards Championship was held.

The championship was organized by the
English Billiards Association and featured
players from England, Scotland, and Australia.

The winner of the tournament was a player
named John Roberts Jr., who became
the first world champion of billiards.

8

One of the most accepted theories is that the term comes from the surname of an English billiards player named Tom Reece.

Reece was one of the first players to consistently apply side spin to the cue ball, and it is said that he used the term "English" to refer to this spin in honor of his country of origin.

Another theory suggests that the term "English" is derived from the English verb "to spin," which means to rotate or cause something to rotate around its axis.

By applying side spin to the cue ball, it rotates around its axis, which could have given rise to the term "English."

In any case, the truth is that the term "English" has been used in the world of billiards for a long time and is an important part of the sport's vocabulary.

9

The red dots found on the cue ball in billiards are known as "reference marks" and serve to help players better visualize the spin and rotation of the ball during play.

The idea of adding the red dots to the cue ball is attributed to the Belgian company Aramith, which manufactures high-quality billiard balls.

The reference mark was designed to make the cue ball more visible and allow players to aim more accurately.

Additionally, the cue ball with red dots is also useful for television viewers watching a billiards match.

The red dots make it easier to follow the movement and trajectory of the cue ball on the screen.

As for the number of red dots on the cue ball, traditionally 6 red dots are used, but some manufacturers may use more or fewer dots depending on the brand or model of the ball.

In summary, the red dots on the cue ball are an important tool in the game of billiards, as they allow players and spectators to better see the rotation and effects of the ball.

10

There are several reasons why snooker tables are so large compared to other billiards games.

Firstly, snooker evolved from English billiards, which was played on a larger table than American billiards.

Snooker, therefore, inherited this characteristic and kept the larger table.

Secondly, snooker is played with 21 balls, which means more space is needed on the table to accommodate all the balls.

Additionally, the balls are smaller than those used in American billiards, so they need more space to move around and for the game to be fair.

Another reason why snooker tables are large is that the game requires a high degree of precision and skill.

The larger table provides an additional challenge for players, making the game more exciting and demanding.

Furthermore, the table size allows players to play a wider variety of shots and strategies, adding more complexity to the game.

11

In the international rules of American pool, the two-shot rule is not used.

The two-shot rule is used in some variants of billiards, such as in blackball, where after committing a foul, the incoming player has two shots to try to resolve the situation.

On the first shot, the player can place the cue ball in any position behind the head string, and on the second shot, they must play from where they left the cue ball on the first shot.

In other games, such as snooker, the two-shot rule is also used in specific situations.

12

The number 4 ball in American pool is usually purple, not lilac.

However, in some ball sets, such as the Aramith Pro Cup TV set, ball 4 is pink instead of purple to improve its visibility on television and avoid confusion with other balls.

It is a common practice in televised billiards to change the color of certain balls so they can be better distinguished on the screen.

This is also done with the number 12 ball, which in some cases is pink instead of orange to avoid confusion with the number 5 ball (yellow).

13

The numbering of the balls in American billiards has its origin in the game of "14.1 continuous" or "straight pool," which became a very popular game in the United States in the late 19th and early 20th centuries.

In this game, players try to reach a predetermined score by making shots and pocketing balls.

The balls are re-racked after each turn and can be pocketed in any order.

With the large number of balls used in this game, a numbering system was necessary to keep track of the pocketed balls.

From there, the numbering spread to other American billiard games, such as 8-ball and 9-ball.

In contrast, in snooker and other billiard games, the colors of the balls are used to differentiate them.

In snooker, for example, the red balls are worth one point each, while the colored balls are worth two to seven points each.

Additionally, the location of the colored balls on the table is fixed, which means that players do not need numbering to keep track of the pocketed balls.

14

The green color of snooker tables is a tradition that dates back to the early days of the sport.

Originally, green was used because green grass was common on croquet courts where the precursor to snooker was played.

As snooker evolved and moved into enclosed billiard rooms, the green color was maintained as a tradition.

On the other hand, the blue color of American pool tables is more recent.

In the 1960s, Brunswick introduced blue chalk as an alternative to traditional green chalk and at the same time introduced blue pool tables to complement the new chalk.

Since then, blue has become a standard in American pool, although green tables can still be found in some locations and competitions.

15

Snooker players use a technique called "sighting" to calculate shots off cushions.

This technique involves aligning the object ball (the one to be hit) with the white ball and the point where the object ball is to hit the cushion.

Players use their imagination to visualize the shot line and the trajectory of the object ball after contact with the cushion.

In addition, experienced players also use their previous knowledge and experience to adjust their shot according to the conditions of the table and the speed of the ball.

16

Tilting the cue in billiards is a technique used by players to apply spin or English to the cue ball upon impact with the target ball.

Tilting the cue to the left or right, depending on which hand the player is holding the cue in, allows for applying a side spin or English to the cue ball.

The cue can also be tilted up or down to apply backspin or follow to the cue ball, respectively.

However, tilting the cue too much can result in a bad shot or even a foul, especially if the cue is not in contact with the cue ball upon impact.

Therefore, it is important for players to learn how to tilt the cue in a controlled and precise manner, which requires practice and skill.

More experienced players can even apply multiple spins at the same time, allowing them to make more complex and challenging shots.

17

The position of the backhand in billiards is crucial for achieving good technique and accuracy in the shot.

The backhand, also known as the "support hand," should not grip the cue too tightly or too loosely but should have a comfortable and relaxed grip.

The backhand should be in a comfortable and stable position, supported on the billiard table, with fingers extended and slightly curved upwards.

The grip on the cue should be gentle, allowing for a free and fluid movement of the arm when making the stroke.

When making the stroke, the backhand should remain stable in its position and not move during the arm movement.

It should serve as a firm support point to maintain balance and stability of the body during the shot.

18

Foot position is crucial in billiards.

A correct stance with feet shoulder-width apart and the front foot slightly inclined forward helps to have a stable balance and good alignment of the body with the cue.

If the feet are too close together, balance is lost and the posture is less stable, which can negatively affect the shot.

In addition, it is important for the feet to be parallel to the line of the shot to ensure that the body is aligned correctly and not twisted.

The position of the front foot can vary slightly according to personal preferences and shooting technique, but it is generally recommended to be slightly inclined forward to help maintain balance.

It is also important to note that the feet should be firmly planted on the ground and not move during the shot, as this can negatively affect the accuracy of the stroke.

It is common for players to sway slightly back and forth while aiming, but it is important to avoid sudden or excessive movements that can unbalance the body.

Finally, it is important to have a relaxed and comfortable stance to avoid muscle tension, which can affect shot accuracy.

It is important to find a stance that feels natural and comfortable and make small adjustments as needed to improve alignment and balance.

19

The reason why the white ball comes out again after falling into a pocket is because the game continues, and the white ball is necessary to keep playing.

If the white ball didn't come out of the pocket after being sunk, the player would have to take another white ball from their pocket or from the rack to keep playing.

In the case of pool, where the white ball is larger than the other balls, there are no magnets or metal particles inside it.

An extra white ball is simply used to continue the game.

In other billiard games, such as snooker, the white ball does not come out of the pocket but the player places it in a specific position on the table to continue playing.

20

Thomas Jefferson, the third President of the United States, had a billiard table in his home at Monticello in Virginia.

However, there is no conclusive evidence that the reason he placed it in the dome of his house was to hide it because billiards was illegal at that time.

Although it is true that in some places in the United States during the 18th and early 19th centuries, billiards was considered a game of chance and therefore prohibited.

However, legislation varied from place to place and it is unclear whether it was illegal or not in Virginia, where Jefferson lived.

In any case, it is not uncommon for someone in Jefferson's position to want to enjoy billiards, as it was a very popular game at the time and was considered an elegant form of entertainment.

Additionally, there are records of other important figures of the time, such as George Washington, also playing billiards.

Jefferson's billiard table in the dome of Monticello is an example of the passion for this game in the history of the United States and an example of the ingenuity and creativity that some people can show to enjoy their favorite pastimes.

21

According to a study by Stanford University in 2014, billiards champions have the highest average age compared to champions of other sports.

The study analyzed the average age of champions in 44 different sports and found that the billiards champion had an average age of 35.6 years.

It is believed that one of the reasons why billiards champions are older is because the game requires a lot of skill and experience.

It often takes a long time to develop the necessary technique and strategy to be a successful billiards player.

Additionally, billiards players tend to have longer and more successful careers than athletes in other sports, allowing them to compete at a high level for a longer period of time.

22

In the 15th century, Louis XI of France had a domestic table with grass placed on top of it, which was used to play the jeu de mail.

This table is considered a precursor to billiards, as a ball and stick were used to strike it, although it did not have the holes or pockets characteristic of modern billiards.

23

It is believed that the first modern billiards room was built in England in 1765.

This place was called "St. James's Billiards Room" and was located on Jermyn Street in London.

This billiards room was founded by a man named Joseph Elmer, who had a great interest in the game and saw the commercial potential of creating a room dedicated solely to billiards.

The room quickly became a popular spot for billiards players of the time, including nobility and aristocrats.

St. James's Billiards Room was also known as the place where snooker was first created and played in 1875 by British army officer Neville Chamberlain.

24

Most "chalks" for billiard cues are not made of real chalk, but of a compound of limestone powder or magnesium silicate.

This compound is known as "billiard chalk" and is used to create a rough surface on the tip of the cue that increases friction and helps prevent the tip from slipping when striking the ball.

The reason abrasives are used instead of real chalk is that chalk is a relatively soft material and wears down quickly when rubbed against the cue tip.

Billiard chalk, on the other hand, is more durable and provides better grip on the cue tip.

It should be noted that real chalk can still be found for billiard cues, but its use is much less common than billiard chalk.

Real chalk has the advantage of not leaving residue on the table, but it must be applied more frequently than billiard chalk due to its tendency to wear down more quickly.

25

In the 1860s, some billiards players ate chalk to relieve stomach pain.

The chalk used at that time was made of calcium carbonate, which was also used as a home remedy for stomach problems.

However, today's billiard chalk is made of other ingredients, such as calcium sulfate or silica, and its consumption is not recommended.

In addition, eating chalk can cause health problems, such as irritation of the respiratory and digestive tract.

Therefore, it is important to use chalk only for its intended purpose: to improve grip on the cue ball and reduce slippage.

26

Roy Motes' feat is considered one of the most impressive in the history of billiards.

In the 1916 National 3-Cushion Championship, Motes did something that no player had achieved before: on his first break shot, he pocketed seven balls in a row, which is known as a "seven in a row."

This achievement is not only impressive because of the difficulty of making seven consecutive shots without missing, but also because at that time billiard tables were much larger and cues were heavier and more difficult to handle than those used today.

Motes' feat has been remembered as one of the great moments in billiards history and has inspired many players to try to equal his achievement.

27

In standard 8-ball, the balls are arranged in a triangular formation in the bottom half of the billiard table, with the 8-ball located at the center of the formation and the head ball (number 1) located at the tip of the triangle.

The striped balls (1-7) must be placed in the bottom half of the triangle, while the solid balls (9-15) must be placed in the top half.

The remaining balls (2, 3, 4, 5, 6, 7, and 8) can be placed in any manner inside the triangle.

Additionally, on the opening break shot, the player breaking must strike the 1-ball from behind the head string, which is an imaginary line located at the top of the table, parallel to the short rails and dividing the top half of the table from the bottom half.

If a player pockets a ball on the break, they continue to play, and their choice of group (stripes or solids) is determined by the first ball they make.

If they do not pocket a ball on the break, their opponent takes their turn.

28

In the game of 9-ball, the balls are arranged in a triangle at the bottom of the billiard table, with the number 1 ball in the front position, at the tip of the triangle, and the other balls placed in a specific pattern behind it.

The 9-ball is placed in the center of the triangle, surrounded by the 8-ball and the 10-ball at the two ends of the triangle.

The placement of the balls in the triangle must follow a specific pattern.

The end balls must be one striped ball and one solid ball in any order, followed by the number 2 ball.

The remaining balls are placed randomly inside the triangle.

It is important to make sure that the balls are tight and in contact with each other to prevent them from moving easily during play.

Once the balls are placed in the triangle, the triangle rack should be carefully removed without moving the balls.

Then, the game begins.

29

Chalk is used in billiards to prevent the cue tip from slipping when striking the ball, providing greater friction and grip.

The history of chalk in billiards dates back to the early 19th century, when players began looking for a way to improve cue grip.

It is said that the first type of chalk used in billiards was ordinary chalk, but it was quickly discovered that it did not provide enough grip and wore out quickly.

In 1897, a player named William Spinks created a special billiard chalk that contained barium sulfate, a chemical compound that provided greater grip and durability.

30

There are different types of chalk used in billiards, although the most common are blue and green.

- Blue chalk: This is the most commonly used chalk in billiards. It is made from calcium carbonate, chalk, and blue pigments. Blue chalk tends to stain the table cloth less and usually lasts longer on the cue.

- Green chalk: This chalk is made from calcium carbonate, chalk, and green pigments. It is said that the green pigment particles in the chalk can adhere more strongly to the table cloth, which can make the cloth get dirty faster and wear out more quickly.

- Red chalk: It is less common and is usually used in some billiard competitions, especially in snooker. Red chalk is made from iron oxide and calcium carbonate, which gives it its distinctive red color.

In addition to these traditional chalks, there are also some innovative chalks that offer different benefits.

For example, some chalks contain silicone or other ingredients that help reduce friction between the cue and the ball, which can help avoid unwanted effects and improve accuracy.

31

The table cloth is an essential part of any billiard table, and its choice can significantly affect the game.

Table cloths are available in a wide variety of materials, colors, and prices.

Some of the most common materials used in the manufacture of billiard table cloths are wool, polyester, and wool-polyester blends.

Billiard table cloths can vary in their speed and ball retention capacity.

The type of table cloth used will depend on the type of game being played.

For example, the cloth used on a carom table will be different from the cloth used on a pool or snooker table.

The composition of billiard table cloths can be divided into several types:

- The 90% combed wool and 10% polyamide cloth is used for playing 3-cushion carom and is one of the best choices for billiard professionals worldwide.

- The 80% combed wool and 20% polyamide cloth is the most economical choice suitable for both carom and pool, and is the most used for home tables.

- The 85% combed wool and 15% polyamide cloth is the preference of pool professionals, as it ensures long life without limiting speed or consistency.

- The 100% carded wool cloth is the professional choice for snooker play and has short, stiff directional pile.

- The 95% carded wool and 5% polyamide cloth is used for English pool on 6 and 7-foot tables.

32

The World Pool Championship is the most important pool tournament in the world and is held annually in Las Vegas, Nevada.

The tournament is organized by the Association of Professional Billiards and Pool (APBP) and features a variety of disciplines, including 8-ball, 9-ball, and straight pool.

The championship brings together the world's best pool players and offers a large cash prize, which varies depending on the discipline.

The cash prize for the winner of the 8-ball discipline is $40,000, while the winner of the 9-ball discipline takes home $50,000.

The cash prize for the winner of the straight pool discipline is $30,000.

In addition, the winner of the overall World Pool Championship also takes home an additional cash prize.

Doubles and team tournaments are also held at the World Pool Championship.

The doubles tournament offers a cash prize of $10,000 for first place, while the team tournament offers a cash prize of $30,000 for first place.

In summary, the World Pool Championship is a very important pool event that attracts the world's best players and offers large cash prizes.

33

The World Carom Championship is the most important carom tournament in the world, also known as the UMB (World Billiards Union) World Billiards Championship.

It is held annually in different countries, although in recent years it has been held in South Korea.

The tournament features several game modes, including three-cushion, four-cushion, and five-cushion.

At the World Carom Championship, players compete in direct elimination matches, where the winner advances to the next round.

The cash prize varies depending on the game mode and the tournament edition, but in general, the total prize money ranges between 100,000 and 300,000 US dollars.

Players can also earn points for the world carom ranking based on their performance in the tournament.

The most successful players in the history of the World Carom Championship include Torbjorn Blomdahl from Sweden, who has won the tournament nine times, and Dick Jaspers from the Netherlands, who has won the tournament seven times.

Other notable players include Semih Sayginer from Turkey, Frederic Caudron from Belgium, and Eddy Merckx from Belgium.

34

The Mosconi Cup is a pool tournament in which teams from Europe and the United States compete.

The tournament is named after the legendary American pool player, Willie Mosconi.

The competition is held annually in December and lasts for four days.

The event is held in a series of individual and team matches, and the first team to win 11 matches is crowned as the winner of the Mosconi Cup.

The tournament is known for its competitive and exciting atmosphere and is very popular among pool fans.

The competition features some of the world's best pool players, including Shane Van Boening, Earl Strickland, and Darren Appleton.

In terms of prizes, the Mosconi Cup has significantly increased its prize pool in recent years.

In 2021, the total prize pool was $225,000, with $30,000 designated for the player on the winning team.

35

The US Open Nine-Ball Championship is one of the most prestigious pool tournaments in the world and is held annually in the United States.

The tournament is played in the 9-ball format and features a large prize pool.

The first tournament was held in 1976 and has been won by some of the greatest pool players of all time, including Earl Strickland, Efren Reyes, Johnny Archer, and Shane Van Boening.

In the 2021 edition, the prize pool was $375,000, with $50,000 awarded to the winner.

The tournament is played over several days and features a group stage followed by a knockout stage.

Players must qualify for the event or be invited to participate.

The US Open Nine-Ball Championship is considered one of the most important events on the pool calendar and attracts a large audience worldwide.

36

The World Cup of Pool is a double-elimination format pool tournament where teams of two players from different countries compete.

It was created in 2006 and is held annually in London, England.

The tournament is organized by Matchroom Sport, a sports events company, and has a large audience worldwide.

In the World Cup of Pool, each team competes in a series of 9-ball matches until only one team is left standing.

The event has been won by teams from different countries, including the Philippines, China, Germany, Taiwan, and Austria.

The prize pool of the World Cup of Pool has varied over the years but is generally quite high.

In the last edition of the tournament in 2019, the prize pool was $250,000, with $60,000 awarded to the winning team.

Teams that reach the semifinals also receive cash prizes.

37

The Derby City Classic is an annual billiards event held in Louisville, Kentucky.

It features a wide variety of disciplines, including 9-ball, 10-ball, straight pool, one pocket, bank pool, and several other game formats.

The event takes place over several days and is known for its festive atmosphere and for attracting some of the world's best billiards players.

Regarding prizes, the prize pool of the Derby City Classic varies depending on the discipline and the player's final position in the tournament.

For example, in the 9-ball tournament, the first place can receive a prize of up to $16,000, while the second place can receive $8,000.

In the one pocket tournament, the first place can receive a prize of up to $12,000, while the second place can receive $6,000.

The Derby City Classic also features several secondary and sponsor events that offer additional prizes.

Overall, the prize pool of the event usually exceeds $300,000.

38

The Women's World Pool Championship is one of the most important tournaments in the world of women's billiards.

The event is organized by the World Pool-Billiard Association (WPA) and attracts some of the best female players from around the world.

The tournament format can vary each year, but generally includes several pool disciplines, such as 9-ball and 10-ball.

The event is held in different locations each year, including China, the United States, and the Philippines.

As for the prize purse, it can vary from year to year, but is usually significant.

For example, at the 2019 Women's World Pool Championship held in Shenyang, China, the total prize was $194,000 USD, with $43,000 USD going to the individual winner.

39

Checking the level of the pool table is an important part of regular pool table maintenance to ensure fair and consistent gameplay.

If the table is tilted or unbalanced, balls can roll unevenly and affect the game.

There are several ways to check the level of the pool table.

One common way is to use a leveling tool, which is placed at different points on the table to measure its tilt.

The leveling tool has a bubble that moves towards the center when the table is level.

The points measured are generally the four corners and the center of the table.

Another way to check the level of the table is by using billiard balls.

A ball is placed in each corner of the table and the distance between the ball and the table is checked to see if it's level.

If there is a significant difference in distance, the table may be unbalanced.

It's important to note that checking the table level should be done by a professional if adjustments are needed.

If the table is unbalanced, adjustments can be made to the legs or shims under the table to level it properly.

40

Maintaining your pool table in good condition is important to ensure fair gameplay and a long lifespan of the table.

-Regularly clean the table surface: The table surface should be cleaned regularly to prevent dirt and dust buildup. To do this, a pool table brush or a soft, damp cloth can be used.

-Do not leave heavy objects on the table: Heavy objects should not be placed on the pool table as they can deform the surface and affect the game. Additionally, avoid placing hot objects on the table, such as food dishes or hot beverages, as they can leave stains or damage the cloth.

-Cover the table when not in use: Covering the table when not in use is an effective way to protect it from dust and dirt buildup, as well as protect the cloth from UV rays.

-Maintain the table cloth: The table cloth is one of the most important parts of the pool table, so it's important to keep it in good condition. It's recommended to regularly brush the cloth with a special pool table brush to prevent dirt and dust buildup.

-Regularly check the table rails: The pool table rails can wear out over time and affect gameplay. The rails should be checked regularly for loose or worn-out rails and replaced if necessary.

-Keep the table level: A level pool table is crucial for fair and accurate gameplay. It's important to regularly check the table level and adjust it as necessary. A leveling tool can be used for this.

-Maintain proper humidity: Pool tables should be kept in an environment with proper humidity to prevent the surface from drying out and cracking. A humidity between 40% and 60% is recommended.

41

French billiards.

Also known as carom billiards, is a variant of
billiards played with three balls on a
table without pockets.

The objective of the game is to make the player's
ball hit the other two balls (the opponent's
ball and the red ball) in a sequence
of caroms to score points.

French billiards has several disciplines, including
three-cushion, four-cushion, and five-cushion,
which refer to the number of times the player's
ball must hit the table's cushions before
hitting the other two balls.

French billiards is very popular in Europe and has
been a recognized sport by the International
Billiards Federation since 1952.

42

English billiards.

Known as pocket billiards, is a variant of billiards played
with three balls: a white ball, a yellow ball, and a red ball.

The objective of the game is to hit the white ball so that it hits
the other two balls and make caroms, i.e., hit both balls
in a single play without committing fouls.

English billiards is played on a rectangular table with
six pockets, three on each end of the table.

Each pocket is located in the corner and middle
of each long side of the table.

The game starts with the placement of the three balls
in the starting position at one end of the table.

The first player hits the white ball to try to make a carom.

If the player fails to make a carom, the turn
passes to the other player.

English billiards is a game of precision and strategy, as players
must plan their shots to make caroms and prevent the
opponent from having opportunities to score points.

The game also has specific rules about fouls, including
touching the wrong ball, not making contact with
the other balls, and hitting a ball off the table.

43

Snooker.

It is a game of precision and strategy played on a regulation size billiard table (12 feet by 6 feet) with six pockets in the corners and middle of each side.

The objective of the game is to score more points than the opponent by potting the balls into the pockets on the table.

The game is played with 21 balls, including 15 red balls, 6 different colored balls (yellow, green, brown, blue, pink, and black), and a white ball used to hit the other balls.

Each player starts their turn by trying to pot a red ball and then a colored ball. If they pot a ball, they earn the corresponding points and their turn continues.

If they fail to pot a ball, they lose their turn, and their opponent starts their turn.

After all the red balls have been potted, players must pot the colored balls in a specific order, and the points awarded vary depending on the color of the ball.

The game requires skill in the technique of hitting the white ball and controlling the direction and speed of the ball, as well as strategy to plan the next shot and anticipate the opponent's moves.

Snooker is particularly popular in the UK and other English-speaking countries and is considered one of the most difficult sports to master.

Professional players compete in major tournaments like the World Snooker Championship, held annually in Sheffield, England, and attracting a large audience worldwide.

As for its history, snooker originated in British India in the 1870s, and it is believed to have been based on popular board games in the region.

The name "snooker" was derived from a colloquial word used in the British army to describe novice recruits or those who were inexperienced.

In the following years, the game became popular in Great Britain and spread around the world.

44

American pool.

Also known as "pool," it is a variation of billiards played with 16 balls: 15 numbered balls from 1 to 15, and a white ball.

The objective of the game is to use the white ball to hit the numbered balls and sink them into the six pockets of the table in a specific order.

There are various disciplines of pool, including 8-ball, 9-ball, 10-ball, and straight pool.

8-ball is the most popular game, played with 15 balls and the white ball.

The objective is to sink all the balls in your group (stripes or solids) and then the number 8 ball to win the game.

9-ball is another popular game, where only the balls numbered 1 to 9 are used and the objective is to hit the lowest numbered ball first and continue until the number 9 ball.

The player who sinks the number 9 ball wins the game.

Pool is very popular worldwide and played both recreationally and professionally.

There are many important pool tournaments, including the World Pool Championship and the US Open Nine-Ball Championship, which offer large cash prizes for players.

45

Bumper pool.

It is a variation of billiards played on a smaller table with obstacles in the form of bumpers or cushions in the center of the table.

The objective of the game is to hit the colored balls towards the pockets at the opposite end of the table, using the bumpers to make challenging shots.

Bumper pool is a game that requires skill and strategy and can be played with two players or in teams of two.

The bumper pool table is generally square, with a length of 121.9 cm and a width of 61 cm.

Unlike traditional billiards, bumper pool has specific rules for the opening shot and the balls in play.

Additionally, the game is known for its fast-paced and exciting play, with challenging shots and tricks that can be used to deceive opponents.

46

Italian or pin billiards.

It is a tabletop game that originated in Italy
in the 18th century.

It is also known as "boccette" or "nine-pin game."

The game is played on a rectangular table with nine pins
arranged in a diamond shape in the center of the table.

Players use two white balls and a red ball.

The objective of the game is to hit the white ball to
strike the pins and knock down as many as possible.

The player who manages to knock down all nine pins
in the fewest number of shots wins the game.

There are also additional points that can be earned
by hitting the red ball or achieving certain
combinations of hits on the pins.

Italian billiards is popular in Italy and other European
countries, although it is not as common in
other parts of the world.

There are competitions and tournaments for Italian
billiards, and various variations of the game
have been developed.

47

Spanish billiards, also known as three-cushion billiards, is a discipline of billiards played with three balls and a table with six pockets.

The objective of the game is to hit both balls with the help of a third ball, so that the player's ball impacts three cushions before touching the other ball, and ultimately enters one of the pockets of the table.

Unlike snooker, Spanish billiards does not have a specific number of red and colored balls, but is played with three numbered balls.

In addition, unlike American billiards, there are no clear divisions between types of play, although the most popular modality is three-cushion billiards.

Spanish billiards is very popular in Europe, especially in countries like Spain, France, Italy, and Belgium.

It is also recognized by the European Billiards Union (UEB) and the World Confederation of Billiards (UMB) as a discipline of billiards.

Spanish billiards has produced great players and legends such as Spanish player Antonio Ortiz, Belgian player Raymond Ceulemans, French player Torbjörn Blomdahl, among others.

It also has important events and tournaments, such as the UMB World Three-Cushion Championship and the King's Cup of Billiards.

48

Belgian billiards, also known as pyramid, is a variant of billiards played mainly in Belgium and other countries in Eastern Europe.

In this game, 15 red balls and one white ball are used, and the objective is to sink as many red balls as possible in the six pockets of the table before sinking the white ball.

The billiard table for pyramid is larger than the tables used for pool or snooker, and the pockets are smaller.

Additionally, the balls are arranged in a triangle at the top of the table, instead of a triangle at the bottom half of the table, as in pool.

The game also has different rules regarding fouls and shots, and a scoring system based on the number of balls sunk.

In some countries, such as Russia, pyramid is considered a national sport and regular local, regional, and national competitions are organized.

49

Indian billiards, also known as Hindu pool or simply Hindu, is a variant of billiards played mainly in India and other countries in South Asia.

Unlike other billiard variants, Hindu is played with only three balls: two red balls and one white ball.

The objective of the game is to hit the two red balls with the white ball and sink them in the six pockets of the board.

The Hindu billiard board is similar to other billiard games but has six pockets instead of four.

The game is played on a rectangular board with dimensions of 10 feet x 5 feet (304.8 cm x 152.4 cm).

The game is typically played in a points format, where each player tries to accumulate as many points as possible.

Players take turns and receive one point for each red ball they sink in a pocket.

If a player sinks both red balls in one shot, they receive two points.

The first player to reach a predefined number of points wins the game.

Hindu billiards is a popular game in India and other countries in South Asia and is played both recreationally and in competitions.

Although not as well-known in other countries, there have been efforts to promote it internationally, and there have been international Hindu billiard competitions in countries such as France and Germany.

50

There are different ways to grip a pool cue:

- **Closed fist:** the player holds the cue like a hammer, with the hand firmly wrapped around the handle. This grip can provide a good sense of control, especially for stronger shots, but may limit accuracy on softer or precision shots.

- **Open or semi-open:** involves holding the cue with fingers open or semi-open around the handle. This technique provides greater accuracy on shots and allows for better control of the ball, but may not be as effective on stronger shots.

- **Embracing the cue:** the player wraps their arm around the cue, providing greater control and stability. It is especially useful for precision shots but may be less effective for power shots.

- **Spider technique:** used for shots where the player needs to lift the cue to make contact with the ball. It involves supporting the bridge hand on the table cloth and using a special cue extension known as a spider, which resembles an inverted "Y".

- **Hammer grip:** this is a common grip where the cue is held like a hammer, with the hand wrapped around the bottom of the handle. It is a comfortable grip for beginners but may limit accuracy and power of the shot.

- **Open bridge grip:** in this grip, the index and middle fingers are extended to create a "V" that is placed on the table, while the rest of the hand holds the cue handle. This grip allows for greater range of motion and can be useful for long distance shots.

- **Closed bridge grip:** similar to the open bridge grip, but instead of extending the fingers, they are brought together to form a closed bridge. This provides a more stable surface to support the cue and is useful for precision shots.

- **Open hand grip:** the hand wraps around the cue handle and the fingers extend upwards to create an additional point of contact with the cue. This can provide better control over the cue's impact angle and is useful for delicate shots.

- **Closed hand grip:** the hand wraps around the cue handle with the fingers pointing downwards. This can provide more power in the shot, but may be difficult to control for precision shots.

51

Tips to help you improve at billiards:

- **Practice regularly:** Billiards is a sport that requires a lot of practice to improve. Dedicate regular time to playing and practicing.

- **Pay attention to body position:** Body position is very important in billiards. Maintain a stable posture and make sure you are comfortable to be able to perform movements smoothly.

- **Learn to control the white ball:** The white ball controls the game, so it is important to learn to control it. Pay attention to the speed and force with which you hit the ball and try to practice soft and precise shots.

- **Visualize the shot before executing it:** Before making the shot, visualize the result you want and try to focus on the movement you need to make to achieve it.

- **Work on your mental focus:** Billiards is a game that requires good mental focus. Learn to relax and focus on the game, avoid getting distracted by other stimuli.

- **Seek the help of a coach or mentor:** A coach or mentor can help you identify your strengths and weaknesses and give you specific advice on how to improve.

- **Play with better players than you:** Playing with more experienced and skilled players than you can help you learn new techniques and strategies, and also give you the opportunity to practice at a higher level.

- **Maintain a positive attitude:** Keep a positive attitude and don't get discouraged if you don't make a particular shot. Billiards is a game of practice and patience, so keep working and having fun.

52

Juan David Zapata is a Colombian billiards player born on December 23, 1997 in the municipality of San Francisco, Antioquia.

Although he began playing at the age of 13, his professional career began to take off in 2017 when he won the gold medal in the Youth World Billiards Championship in China, in the discipline of 9-ball.

Since then, Zapata has had great success in the world of billiards, standing out for his skill in various disciplines, including 8-ball, 9-ball, and straight pool.

In 2019, he became the champion of the International Billiards Open in Mexico, one of the most important tournaments in Latin America.

In the same year, Zapata won the gold medal in the Pan American Games in Lima in the 9-ball discipline, becoming the first Colombian player to win a gold medal in billiards in this competition.

In addition, he has represented Colombia in several international events, including the World Billiards Cup and the World Billiards League.

53

Chang Jung Lin is a Taiwanese professional billiards player born in 1989.

He is known for his skill in the game of 9-ball and has won several major titles in his career.

Among his most notable achievements are the gold medal in the 2017 Men's World Pool Championship held in Doha, Qatar, and the title of the 2019 US Open 9-Ball in Las Vegas, Nevada.

In addition, he has won several tournaments in the World Pool Masters event series and has been ranked among the top players in the world by the International Billiards Federation.

In terms of his playing style, Chang is known for his precise and methodical approach to the billiards table.

He is also recognized for his great skill in controlling the cue ball, allowing him to effectively position the ball for the next play.

54

Dennis Orcollo is a Filipino professional billiards player born on January 8, 1979 in Bisayas, Philippines.

He is considered one of the best pool players today, having won numerous titles and accolades throughout his career.

Orcollo began playing billiards at the age of 8 and became a professional player at 16.

In 2006, he won his first major title at the World Pool Masters in Las Vegas.

Since then, he has won many other major titles, including the 2011 US Open and the 2012 Derby City Classic.

Orcollo has also been a member of the Philippine team in the Mosconi Cup and has been a key player in the Philippines' victory on several occasions.

In addition, he has been named Player of the Year by the World Pool Association twice, in 2011 and 2012.

Orcollo is known for his skill in the 9-ball game and is distinguished by his technique and precision on the table.

He is also recognized for his dedication and discipline in his training, as well as his competitive mindset in tournaments.

55

Shane Van Boening is a professional billiards player born in South Dakota, United States, in 1983.

He is known as one of the best billiards players in the world and has won numerous major titles in his career.

Van Boening started playing billiards at a young age and quickly showed exceptional talent.

In 2007, he won his first major title at the World 10-Ball Championship.

Since then, he has won multiple championships, including five US Open 9-Ball titles, four World 10-Ball Championship titles, and three Derby City Classic World Pool Championship titles.

Additionally, Van Boening has represented the United States team in the Mosconi Cup, an annual pool tournament where teams from Europe and the United States compete.

He has been one of the most successful players in the tournament's history, having won the Player of the Tournament award four times.

Van Boening is known for his skill in 9-Ball, where he is considered one of the world's best players.

He is also known for his focused mentality and ability to handle pressure in high-stress situations.

Regarding his playing style, Van Boening is a very technical and precise player.

He has a smooth and fluid stroke technique, which allows him to execute difficult shots with ease.

He is also known for his ability in jump shots, which has allowed him to make some impressive shots in his career.

56

Jasmin Ouschan is an Austrian professional billiards player born in Klagenfurt, Austria, on April 10, 1986.

She is considered one of the most successful players in the history of billiards and has won numerous titles in different disciplines.

Ouschan started playing billiards at the age of six, and at 16 years old, she had already won her first European title in the 14.1 continuous discipline.

Since then, she has accumulated a long list of successes in billiards.

Among her most notable achievements are:
World Champion in the 9-Ball discipline in 2016.

Two-time European Champion in 9-Ball (2012 and 2013).

Three-time World Champion in the 10-Ball discipline (2007, 2010, and 2012).

Four-time European Champion in the 10-Ball discipline (2008, 2009, 2010, and 2012).

Women's billiards world champion in 2006. Additionally, Ouschan has represented Austria in numerous international billiards competitions, including the 2008 Beijing and 2012 London Olympics.

She has also been named Player of the Year in Europe and the world several times.

Jasmin Ouschan is known for her skill in defense, making her a formidable opponent for any player.

She is also known for her dedication and work ethic, as well as her positive and friendly attitude towards her fellow players.

57

Efren Reyes.

He is a Filipino billiards player born on August 26, 1954 in Pampanga, Philippines.

He is one of the most successful and respected players in the history of pool, and has won numerous important titles throughout his career.

Reyes began playing billiards at the age of five, and since then has developed a reputation as a master of the art of defensive play.

He is known for his ability to make incredibly precise and complicated shots, and for his ability to make the most of every opportunity presented to him.

Among Reyes' most notable achievements are:
9-ball World Champion in 1999, 2004 and 2008.

Association of Professional Billiards and Snooker (APBU) Championship winner in 1999 and 2000.

Winner of the Derby City Classic in 1999, 2004, 2006 and 2010.

One Pocket World Champion in 1999, 2004 and 2006.

Reyes has also represented the Philippines in numerous international billiards competitions, including the Asian Games and the Southeast Asian Games.

In addition to his defensive play skills, Reyes is known for his quiet personality and modesty.

He has often been described as one of the kindest and humblest players on the professional billiards circuit.

58

Earl Strickland.

He is an American billiards player born on June 8,
1961 in Roseboro, North Carolina.

He is known for his strong personality and aggressive style of play,
and is considered one of the best pool players of all time.

Strickland began playing billiards at a young age and
quickly showed great talent for the sport.

In his career, he has won five world pool championships
and many other important titles.

Among Strickland's most notable achievements are: Five-time 9-ball
World Champion (1984, 1987, 1988, 1990 and 1991).

Three-time US Open 9-ball Champion (1984, 1987 and 1993).

World Pool Masters Champion in 1997 and 2000.

Winner of the Derby City Classic multiple times.

In addition to his achievements in the world of pool, Strickland has also
been a standout player in other billiards games, including
14.1 straight pool and one-pocket.

Strickland is known for his controversial personality
and hot temper on the playing field.

He has had some controversial moments during his career, such as
when he threw his cue stick into the audience at the 1995
World Championship after losing a match.

Despite his often polarizing personality, Strickland is widely
respected for his skill and success in pool.

Many consider him to be one of the most talented players to have ever
existed, and his aggressive and fearless style on the playing field
has made him a fan favorite around the world.

59

Ralph Souquet is a German billiards player born on November 10, 1968 in Eschweiler, Germany.

He is known as "The Gentleman" for his smooth playing style and his ability to make difficult shots look easy.

Souquet has been one of the most successful players in the history of pool and has remained at the top of the sport for decades.

Souquet started playing pool at a young age and quickly showed great talent for the sport.

In his career, he has won multiple world pool championship titles and many other important titles.

Among Souquet's most notable achievements are: Three-time world 9-ball champion (1996, 2002, and 2006).

World straight pool champion in 2000.

Three-time US Open 9-ball champion (2002, 2004, and 2011).

Multiple-time European Pool Championship winner.

Multiple-time winner of the World Pool Masters.

In addition to his achievements in the world of pool, Souquet has also represented Germany in international billiards competitions, including the 2004 Athens Olympics.

Souquet is known for his elegant playing style and his ability to perform difficult shots with ease.

He is also known for his hard work ethic and focus on technique and precision.

Off the field, Souquet is known for his kind and respectful personality.

60

Allison Fisher is a billiards player born in England on February 24, 1968.

She is considered one of the greatest billiards players of all time and has won numerous titles in different disciplines of the sport.

Fisher started playing pool at the age of 7 and quickly showed a great talent for the sport.

Throughout her career, Fisher has won 80 world championship titles, including 11 women's world pool championships.

Some of her most notable achievements include: 11-time women's world pool champion (1994, 1996-1999, 2001-2004, 2007, 2009).

Winner of the 2001 World Games.

Four-time European Women's Pool Championship winner.

Women's US Open 9-ball champion in 1996 and 2001.

Multiple-time WPBA Masters Tournament champion.

Fisher is known for her focus on technique and precision, as well as her skill in defensive play.

She is also known for her hard work ethic and dedication to the sport.

Fisher is respected by her colleagues and admired by billiards fans worldwide.

In addition to her success in the world of billiards, Fisher has also competed in snooker competitions and was the first woman to win a match in a professional snooker tournament.

Outside of the playing field, Fisher is known for her kind and charismatic personality.

61

Ronnie O'Sullivan is a snooker player born in England on December 5, 1975.

He is considered one of the most talented and exciting players in the history of snooker and has won multiple world championships.

O'Sullivan started playing snooker at the age of 7 and soon proved to be a prodigy of the sport.

In 1992, at the age of 16, he became the youngest player to win a professional snooker tournament.

Since then, he has won numerous major titles and has set several records in the sport.

Some of O'Sullivan's most notable achievements include: 6-time world snooker champion (2001, 2004, 2008, 2012, 2013, 2020).

7-time Masters snooker champion.

5-time UK Championship champion.

Holder of the record for the most century breaks in the history of snooker.

Holder of the record for the fastest 147-point maximum break in a televised tournament.

O'Sullivan is known for his exciting and aggressive playing style, and his ability to make incredibly difficult shots.

He is also known for his colorful and occasionally eccentric personality off the playing field, which has made him a beloved player among snooker fans.

Despite his success in snooker, O'Sullivan has dealt with personal and emotional issues off the playing field, leading to periods of inactivity and challenges in his career.

However, his skill in snooker and his ability to come back and win major championships have established him as a legendary figure in the sport.

62

Niels Feijen is a professional pool player from the Netherlands born on May 3, 1977.

He is known as "The Terminator" due to his aggressive and determined playing style in pool.

Feijen has had a very successful career in the world of pool, winning multiple titles and being considered one of the most respected players in the sport.

Some of his notable achievements include: 5-time world pool champion, 3-time World Pool Masters champion, 3-time Eurotour champion, and 2-time US Open pool champion.

In addition to these achievements, Feijen has represented the Netherlands in various international competitions and has been a key player on the European team in the Mosconi Cup, one of the most important pool competitions worldwide.

Feijen is known for his aggressive playing style, where he often attempts difficult shots instead of playing defensively.

He is also known for his work ethic and dedication to the sport, which has led him to the top of the world of pool.

63

Thorsten Hohmann is a professional pool player from Germany, born on July 14, 1979.

He is considered one of the best pool players in the world, having won multiple world championship titles and being recognized for his skill in precision shots and safeties.

Some of Hohmann's notable achievements in the world of pool include: 3-time world pool champion, 2-time US Open pool champion, 2-time World Pool Masters champion, 5-time Eurotour champion, and member of the World Billiards Hall of Fame.

Hohmann has also represented Germany in various international competitions, including the World Cup of Pool and the Mosconi Cup.

Hohmann is known for his skill in precision shots, and is particularly adept at cut shots and long distance shots.

He is also known for his ability in safeties, which allows him to control the table and keep his opponent under pressure.

In addition to his technical skills, Hohmann is also known for his work ethic and dedication to the sport.

He is a highly respected player in the world of pool, and has been a key figure in the sport for many years.

64

Pan Xiaoting is a professional billiards player from China, born on February 25, 1982 in the city of Taizhou, Jiangsu province.

She is considered one of the greatest billiards players of all time and has been a key figure in the development of the sport in China.

Some of Pan's notable achievements in the world of billiards include: 12-time Women's World Billiards Championship winner, 2-time World Games champion, 4-time Asian Women's Billiards Championship winner, and gold medalist at the 2006 Asian Games.

Pan has also been recognized for her contribution to the development of billiards in China.

In 2010, she received the CCTV Sports Personality of the Year award in recognition of her success and her role as a sport ambassador.

Pan is known for her skill in defensive play, and is particularly adept at precision shots and safeties.

She is also known for her mental focus and ability to stay calm under pressure.

In addition to her success in billiards, Pan has been an influential figure in promoting the sport and has worked to increase awareness and popularity of billiards worldwide.

She has been a sport ambassador and has helped inspire a new generation of billiards players in China and beyond.

65

Albert Garnier is considered one of the first high-level carom players and a pioneer of modern billiards.

Garnier was a French player who excelled at carom during the 1870s and is credited with developing shooting techniques and strategies that revolutionized the game in his time.

It is also said that Garnier had trouble maintaining a good grip on the cue stick as it slipped in his hands.

Therefore, he decided to apply beeswax to the butt of the cue stick to improve the grip.

This was one of the first documented cases in which a cover or coating was used on the grip area of the cue stick to improve grip.

From this innovation, other players began to experiment with different materials and techniques to improve grip and comfort when playing.

66

Willie Hoppe began his career as a carom player at the tender age of 6 and quickly became one of the best players in the world.

An interesting anecdote in Hoppe's career tells that when he was a child, Hoppe faced American player Al Taylor.

Before the match, Taylor patted the boy's head and told him that if he beat him, he would buy him an ice cream.

At the end of the game, Hoppe defeated Taylor, and he kept his promise to buy him an ice cream.

However, after breaking his cue stick over his knee, Taylor left and was never heard from again.

67

**Billiards has been played by different social
and cultural strata throughout history.**

In the case of the Duchess of Burgundy, she was
likely one of the first noblewomen to be depicted
playing billiards in an engraving, indicating that
the game was already gaining popularity
among the nobility.

On the other hand, the book "The Compleat Gamester"
written by Charles Cotton in 1674 was the first text
to detail the rules and strategies of billiards and
became an essential guide for players of the time.

In addition to the rules, the book also included advice
on how to win bets and how to detect cheats.

The work was a great success in its time and laid
the groundwork for future treatises on
billiards and other games of chance.

68

The story of the Duke Maximilian of Bavaria losing in a game of billiards is a popular legend that has been told in various ways over time.

According to some versions, the Duke lost a large sum of money in a single afternoon of playing, which would now be valued at $3.6 million.

Other versions say it was over a week of playing.

Furthermore, it is not clear if the winner named Barthels was the Duke's assistant or simply a skilled billiard player.

Although it is not certain if this story is entirely true, it is true that billiards has traditionally been a game associated with gambling and chance.

Historically, high-level billiard players were often wealthy aristocrats or members of royalty who could afford to spend long hours at the billiard table.

The game was also often played in gambling halls and gaming houses, making it a popular activity for those who enjoyed betting on games of chance.

69

Gustave de Coriolis (1835-1920) was a prominent French mathematician, engineer, and scientist who made important contributions in various fields of knowledge, such as hydraulics, mechanics, and astronomy.

In 1935, more than fifteen years after his death, his posthumous work "Mathematical Treatise on Billiards" was published, which became a classic of billiards and a reference for players and fans of the game.

In this treatise, Coriolis applied his mathematical and physical knowledge to analyze and improve the technique of the game, as well as to develop new methods and strategies.

Coriolis's work included a large number of diagrams, formulas, and mathematical calculations that allowed players to better understand the physics of the game and the principles behind shots and plays.

Furthermore, his scientific and rigorous approach influenced the way billiards is taught and played around the world.

70

In 1843, in the French city of Maisons-Laffitte, a duel to the death between two men took place after an argument in a game of billiards.

The men, Lenfant and Mellant, agreed to use billiard balls as weapons in the duel.

Lenfant was hit in the head with a ball and died shortly after due to his injuries.

The incident caught the attention of authorities and led to the prohibition of duels in France.

71

Isidro Rivas.

He was a Spanish billiards player and artist,
born in El Vendrell in 1877.

He is credited with creating artistic or fantasy billiards,
a style of play that focuses on making impressive and
complicated shots involving multiple balls and effects.

Rivas, nicknamed "The Poet of Billiards," began playing
billiards from a young age and quickly developed
a unique skill and creativity in the sport.

In 1902, he won the National Three-Cushion Billiards
Championship, and in 1914, he moved to Paris, where
he participated in artistic billiards tournaments and
exhibitions, showcasing his skill and innovative
techniques in shots like "the bridge,"
"the window," and "the roulette."

Rivas also wrote several books about billiards, including
"The Cathedral of Billiards" and "My Great Games," and
founded a billiards academy in Barcelona, where
he taught young players the techniques and
tricks of artistic billiards.

His legacy has been recognized by many as an
influence in the development and popularization
of artistic billiards worldwide.

72

"Rackham's Billiards" was built by real estate magnate Horace Rackham in 1924 and became one of the most famous billiards venues during the golden age of billiards in the United States.

The venue had 109 billiards tables and was designed to be a gathering place for players of all levels, from beginners to professionals.

In addition to the billiards tables, the venue had an exhibition room and a theater where billiards tournaments and events were held.

The venue was in operation until the 1950s, when it closed due to a decline in the popularity of billiards.

73

Monsieur Mingaut, also known as Jules Pierre Billard, was a French billiards player who became one of the best players of his time.

He became famous for inventing the ball rebound effect, also known as "masse," which involves making the ball spin in the opposite direction to which it is hit.

Mingaut, who had spent much of his life in prison, developed the rebound effect while incarcerated.

As the story goes, he had the idea of putting a piece of leather on the tip of his cue to make the ball spin in the opposite direction.

After his release, he became a professional and famous billiards player in France.

The ball rebound effect allowed billiards players to make more complicated and creative shots and became a popular technique in artistic and fantasy billiards.

Mingaut died in 1933, but his legacy in the world of billiards lives on to this day.

74

Joe Davis.

He was a British snooker player born in
1901 in Whitwell, England.

He is considered the founder of the World Snooker
Championship, which he first won in 1927
and subsequently won 14 more times
until his retirement in 1946.

Davis was the first player to achieve a century break in the
World Championship in 1930 and in 1955, he achieved the
first 147 break in a competition, although it was not
officially recognized by the federation until 1982.

In addition to his success in the world championship, Davis
also won several English billiards and British snooker titles.

After his retirement, Davis became a commentator and
organizer of snooker tournaments, and was inducted
into the Snooker Hall of Fame in 1988.

75

George Sutton.

Known as "The One-Armed Billiardist," he was an American billiards player born in 1893 who became a legend in the sport thanks to his incredible skill and dexterity despite losing both arms above the elbows in a train accident when he was 12 years old.

Sutton learned to play billiards using his two stumps and his chin to hold the cue and make shots.

Despite the difficulty of playing with such a severe disability, Sutton became an exceptionally skilled player and accomplished several notable feats in his career.

In 1930, during an exhibition in New York, Sutton made a run of 3,000 in "free carambole," which means he scored 3,000 points without committing a foul in a game where any ball on the table can be hit regardless of its point value.

This feat was widely publicized in the media at the time and is still remembered as one of the most impressive in billiards history.

Sutton continued to play billiards for many years and became an idol and role model for many people with disabilities around the world.

He died in 1954 at the age of 60.

76

Julius Shuster.

He was a famous American billiards player and juggler, known for his ability to pick up and manipulate multiple billiard balls at the same time.

In 1936, Shuster accomplished an impressive feat by picking up 10 billiard balls in each hand and then flipping them up and down without dropping them.

Shuster became famous in the 1930s and 1940s, and made several appearances on television variety shows of the time, where he displayed his skill with billiard balls and other objects.

In addition to his billiards prowess, Shuster was also a renowned juggler and could perform tricks with clubs, rings, and other objects.

In his career, Shuster won several billiards championships and also participated in exhibition tours around the world.

His ability to pick up and manipulate multiple billiard balls is remembered as one of the most impressive feats in the history of the sport.

77

Sam Sicherman, also known as "the horn man", was a billiards player from New York who became famous for his ability to play with the white ball in his mouth.

In 1938, he achieved an impressive feat by pocketing 15 consecutive balls using this unique technique.

Sicherman started playing billiards at a young age and developed his skill of playing with the white ball in his mouth over many years of practice.

To perform this feat, Sicherman held the white ball between his teeth and forcefully expelled it in the direction he wanted it to go.

While this technique was impressive, it was also dangerous, and many billiards players and spectators advised Sicherman against continuing.

However, Sicherman persisted in playing and improving his technique, and eventually achieved the impressive feat of pocketing 15 consecutive balls using only the white ball in his mouth.

This achievement earned him a great deal of recognition and fame in the billiards community, and is remembered as one of the most outstanding achievements in the history of the game.

78

Johnny Layton, born in 1909, was an American professional billiards player who excelled in various disciplines, including pool and three-cushion billiards.

In 1941, he achieved an impressive feat by making four consecutive runs of 70 balls in the 14.1 discipline in four different billiards halls in Illinois.

The feat was accomplished on the same night and in different cities.

The 14.1 discipline, also known as straight pool, is a game in which players try to pocket all the balls on the table in numerical order, starting with the ball number 1 and ending with ball number 14, and then the ball 15 (the black ball) in any pocket.

A run is when a player pockets several balls in one turn.

Layton's achievement was impressive because the 14.1 discipline requires a lot of precision and skill.

Additionally, making four consecutive runs of 70 balls in one night is a remarkable feat.

Layton is remembered as one of the great billiards players of the golden age of billiards in the United States.

79

The "short double" is a shot in which the player's ball hits the target ball, then bounces off one or two cushions before hitting the target ball a second time and finally pocketing it.

In the case of William E. Bell, while attempting to make this shot, the ball jumped off the table, bounced on the floor, and entered another table, in turn hitting a ball on that table and finally pocketing the original target ball.

Such accidents are extremely rare and are often remembered as curious anecdotes in the history of billiards.

80

The 1952 Three-Cushion Billiards World Championship was held at Luna Park in Buenos Aires, Argentina.

The event drew a crowd of 12,000 spectators and took place from October 13 to 19, organized by the Argentine Billiards Union.

It was the first time the championship was held outside of Europe.

The final was played between Belgian René Vingerhoedt and Frenchman Auguste "Gusti" Cornelis, with Vingerhoedt winning by a score of 60-56 in 71 innings.

This championship was historic as it was the first time that electric heating tables were used, which allowed for a more uniform and predictable game and reduced the impact of environmental conditions on the game.

81

The final of the 1985 World Snooker Championship, played between Steve Davis and Dennis Taylor, was one of the most memorable moments in snooker history.

The final was played best of 35 frames, and after three intense days of competition, the match reached the decider (the decisive frame), which was considered one of the greatest sporting moments on television.

During the decider, Dennis Taylor took a lead of 62-44, but Davis tied the score at 62-62.

After a series of exchanges, Taylor had the chance to win the match but missed on the last shot.

Davis then had the opportunity to make his shot and win the match, but also missed, allowing Taylor to return to the table and win the match with a difficult shot on the black ball.

The 1985 World Snooker Championship final was watched by a record audience of 18.5 million viewers on the BBC, becoming one of the most-watched sporting events in the history of the UK.

The exciting final and the tension of the decider have remained in the memory of snooker fans to this day.

82

**Harry Lewis, also known as "The Great Caruso,"
was an American billiards player
known for his unusual style.**

Instead of using a traditional cue stick,
Lewis used his nose to hit the ball.

Despite how strange it seemed, Lewis proved to
be a very talented player and achieved
some impressive feats.

On one occasion, he made a run of 46 balls using
only his nose, making it one of the most surprising
accomplishments in billiards history.

Additionally, Lewis could also make
spectacular shots using his foot or hand.

Despite his peculiar style, Lewis was a highly
respected player in the world of billiards.

83

Jimmy White is a professional snooker player born in England in 1962.

Despite never having won the World Snooker Championship, he is considered one of the greatest players in the history of the sport.

White has reached six finals of the World Snooker Championship, in 1984, 1990, 1991, 1992, 1993, and 1994.

Unfortunately, he lost all of them, earning him the nickname "the perennial runner-up."

The 1994 final was particularly dramatic, as White lost to Stephen Hendry in the final frame, after having led the scoreboard for much of the match.

Despite his lack of success in the World Championship, White has won other important snooker tournaments throughout his career, including the UK Open, the Masters, and the Grand Prix.

He is known for his aggressive playing style and his ability to make great comebacks in difficult situations.

84

Ronnie O'Sullivan's maximum break in the 1997 World Snooker Championship was a historic moment in the sport of snooker.

O'Sullivan took only 5 minutes and 20 seconds to complete the 147-point break, which is the highest possible score in a single visit to the table.

This makes it the fastest maximum break ever recorded in the history of snooker.

During the break, O'Sullivan made every shot with impressive accuracy, and at one point, even played a shot with his left hand.

The audience present at the Crucible Theatre in Sheffield, where the championship was being held, was ecstatic as they watched O'Sullivan make history.

Since then, O'Sullivan has made a total of 15 maximum breaks in his career, setting a record in the sport of snooker.

85

Mark Roberts is a famous British streaker, known for interrupting various sporting events, including the Snooker Embassy final in Sheffield in 2004 and the final round of the English snooker championship in 2008.

In both events, Roberts stripped naked and ran through the venue, interrupting the game and surprising the players and spectators present.

In the Snooker Embassy final, Roberts was arrested by the police and subsequently fined for his behavior.

In addition to these sporting events, Roberts has interrupted other events such as the Oscars and the Super Bowl.

86

The most expensive pool cue in history is called "The Intimidator" and was made by the famous American pool cue manufacturer, Richard Black.

It is made of ebony and curly maple wood, and features ivory and diamond inlaid details.

The cue sold for $150,000 at an auction in 2003, but was later resold in 2014 for $650,000 to an undisclosed buyer.

In addition to its incredible price, the cue is also known for its beauty and exceptional craftsmanship, making it a valuable collector's item for any billiards lover.

87

The Elysium pool table from the Spanish company IXO is one of the most expensive pool tables on the market.

Its design is futuristic, with finishes in glass and aluminum, and has an approximate price of 160,000 euros.

Each Elysium table is custom made and can be personalized with different high-quality finishes and materials.

It also includes LED lighting technology that allows the table to be illuminated in different colors and patterns.

The table also features a high-fidelity integrated sound system and a 32-inch touchscreen to control lighting, music, and other functions.

Only a few units of the Elysium table have been made, making it a unique and exclusive piece.

88

Walter Lindrum is considered one of the greatest billiards players in history.

He was born in Australia in 1898 and began playing billiards at a young age, thanks to the influence of his father and brother.

He soon proved to be a prodigy in the sport and began winning local and national tournaments.

In 1928, Lindrum traveled to England to compete in the World Billiards Championship, where he surprised everyone with his innovative and highly technical playing style.

Lindrum specialized in the three-cushion game, where players must hit the white ball to touch three cushions before hitting the red ball and scoring a point.

His skill in the three-cushion game became legendary, and he became the world champion in the discipline in 1933, a title he held until his retirement in 1950.

Lindrum was also known for his "massé shot," in which he used a lot of spin to make the white ball move backwards after hitting the target ball, allowing him to control the position of the white ball for his next shots.

His skill in this shot made him virtually unbeatable in long matches.

As for the mausoleum, it was built in 1960 after Lindrum's death as a tribute to his life and career in billiards.

The mausoleum is a representation of a billiards table with its balls and cue carved in marble, and is one of the most visited monuments in the cemetery.

89

Billiards is considered the national sport of the Philippines.

In this country, billiards is played in different modalities, but the most popular is called "pool," which is played with 15 numbered balls and a white ball, and is practiced in billiard halls throughout the country.

Filipinos have excelled in this sport and many players from this country have won championships and international recognitions in different billiard modalities, including pool and carom (three-cushion).

One of the most famous Filipino players is Efren Reyes, known as "The Magician," who is considered by many as one of the greatest players in the history of billiards.

90

John Smith is a professional billiards player from the United States and is nicknamed "Mr. 600" because he was the first player in history to exceed 600 consecutive balls in the 14.1 billiards modality.

The previous record was held by the legendary billiards player Willie Mosconi, who had set his mark of 526 consecutive balls in 1954 during an exhibition match against Earl Bruney.

However, there are some differences between both records.

Mosconi's mark was achieved on an 8-foot table, while Smith's was achieved on a 9-foot table.

Additionally, Mosconi achieved his record in an exhibition match against an opponent, while Smith did it without an opponent, only going for the record.

91

The billiard table doesn't know when to return the white ball, but it is thanks to physics that this happens.

When the white ball is struck by the cue, it is transferred a certain amount of kinetic energy that allows it to move.

When the white ball strikes another ball, a portion of that energy is transferred to that ball, while another portion is lost due to friction between the balls and the table.

In the case of the white ball, when it strikes a ball, it loses enough energy to eventually come to a stop and stay at rest on the table.

It is at this moment when the table "returns" the white ball, as its flat and smooth surface allows the ball to roll and move easily.

92

Illuminated balls are a type of billiard balls that have been designed to add a more spectacular and eye-catching touch to the game.

They are equipped with small integrated LED indicators that light up when hit by the cue, when colliding with other balls, or when bouncing off the table's rails.

They are made of acrylic material and are coated with a hardened polymer to cushion the impact.

These balls can be fun to play with in low-light environments or even in nighttime competitions.

However, they are not necessary to play billiards effectively and are not allowed in most official competitions.

As for the billiard cue laser pointer, it is another game accessory that helps players achieve better accuracy when hitting the white ball.

The laser emits a red beam of light that points to the exact spot where the player should hit the ball to achieve the desired effect.

Like illuminated balls, this accessory is not essential to play billiards, but it can be fun to experiment with.

93

Therese Klompenhouwer is a professional billiards player from the Netherlands, born on October 22, 1982.

She is considered one of the best three-cushion billiards players in the sport's history and has won numerous championships and titles throughout her career.

She started playing billiards at the age of 6 and won her first Dutch championship at the age of 16.

Since then, she has won seven individual European three-cushion championships and three individual World three-cushion championships, in 2011, 2014, and 2018.

In addition to her individual success, Klompenhouwer has been an integral part of the Dutch billiards team, helping to win several European and World team championships.

In 2017, she became the first woman to play in the Dutch professional men's billiards league.

Klompenhouwer has also been recognized for her work in promoting billiards and women's participation in the sport.

Her playing technique is highly regarded by experts in the sport, being recognized for her accuracy, control of the game's pace, and ability to make difficult shots.

94

Karen Corr is a professional billiards player born in Northern Ireland in 1969.

She started playing billiards at the age of 14 and quickly excelled in this sport.

In 1990, she moved to the United States to pursue her career as a professional billiards player and joined the Women's Professional Billiards Association (WPBA) tour in 1991.

Throughout her career, Karen Corr has won numerous titles, including six WPBA world championships and five US Open Billiards titles.

She has also been inducted into the WPBA Billiards Hall of Fame and has been named WPBA Player of the Year four times.

Corr is known for her precise playing style and her ability to control the white ball, as well as her calm and reserved attitude at the table.

She is considered one of the best billiards players of all time and has been a great influence for billiards players worldwide.

95

Jennifer Barretta is an American professional pool player and television personality born in 1979 in Pennsylvania.

She began playing pool at the age of 12 and became a professional at the age of 21.

She is known for her aggressive playing style and her skills in both nine-ball and eight-ball games.

Barretta has won several major titles in her career, including the U.S. National Billiards Championship in 2003 and 2012, the WPBA Women's Championship in 2010, and the WPBA Fastest Shooter Masters in 2011.

She has also been a member of the United States team in the Pool Americas Cup.

In addition to her career as a pool player, Barretta has appeared on several television shows, including hosting the billiards competition show "The Hustlers" on truTV and competing on the show "The Amazing Race" on CBS.

She has also appeared in commercials and television programs as a pool expert.

Barretta is also known for her activism in promoting women's pool and encouraging women's participation in the sport.

In 2013, she founded "The National Billiard Academy," an organization that offers pool classes and training programs for players of all levels.

96

Jeanette Lee, also known as "The Black Widow," is an American professional pool player and television personality born in 1971 in Brooklyn, New York.

She is one of the most successful and famous pool players in the sport's history, having won more than 30 national and international titles in her career.

Lee began playing pool at the age of 18 and became a professional in 1991.

In her career, she has won multiple major championships, including the Women's World 9-Ball Championship in 1998 and 2003, the World Winter Ball Championship in 1998 and 2001, and the Derby City Classic in 2004 and 2007.

In addition to her success on the pool table, Lee has become a popular television personality thanks to her appearances on various pool programs and competitions, as well as other television shows such as "The Apprentice" and "Celebrity Wife Swap."

She has also been an advocate and spokesperson for the Lupus Foundation of America, having been diagnosed with the disease in 1999.

In 2020, Lee publicly revealed that she had been diagnosed with stage 4 breast cancer.

After an intense battle with the disease, she passed away on July 17, 2021, at the age of 49, leaving a legacy as one of the world's most iconic and beloved pool players.

97

Ewa Laurance is a professional billiards player from Sweden, born on February 26, 1964 in Gävle, Sweden.

Also known as "The Striking Viking," Laurance is one of the most successful billiards players in the sport's history.

Laurance began playing billiards at the age of 14 at a local youth center in her hometown.

She soon realized her natural talent for the game and began competing in local tournaments.

At the age of 17, she moved to the United States to play on the professional circuit and began winning major titles.

Throughout her career, Laurance has won over 60 national and international billiards championships, including 4 world titles in different disciplines of the sport.

She has also been inducted into the World Billiards Hall of Fame in 2004 and the Professional Billiards Association Hall of Fame in 2013.

In addition to her playing career, Laurance has also worked as a television commentator and has appeared on several television programs such as "Late Night with David Letterman" and "Real Sports with Bryant Gumbel."

She has also appeared in several movies and television shows, including Martin Scorsese's "The Color of Money" and CBS's "The Equalizer."

Laurance is known for her aggressive playing style and her ability to make incredible shots.

She is also an active advocate for the sport and has worked to promote billiards as a serious and respected sport worldwide.

98

The most expensive billiard ball in the world was auctioned off in 2019 by the auction house Sotheby's in Hong Kong for an impressive amount of $275,000.

The billiard ball in question was the number 4 ball from a limited edition billiard set handmade by the British company John Parris.

The complete billiard set, which consisted of 8 balls, was created in collaboration with snooker and pool player Ronnie O'Sullivan and was presented at the China International Fair in 2016.

The number 4 ball, considered the most valuable of the set, is made of ivory and features diamond and ruby inlays.

It also has Ronnie O'Sullivan's signature engraved on it.

It is worth noting that the use of ivory in the production of billiard balls is prohibited in many countries due to concerns about elephant poaching.

For this reason, many billiard companies now produce balls with synthetic materials instead of ivory.

99

Superstitions and quirks: Tony Drago.

He is a Maltese professional billiard player who has been nicknamed "The Tornado of Malta" for his fast and aggressive playing style.

In addition to his skill in the game, Drago is also known for being very superstitious.

One of Drago's most well-known superstitions is that he always carries a gold coin in his pocket while playing.

According to him, this brings him luck and helps him stay focused.

Drago is also known for being very particular about the cleanliness of the billiard table before each match.

He believes that if the table is not clean, he will not be able to play well.

Another one of Drago's quirks is that he always uses the same chalk for his cue throughout the entire game.

If he loses the chalk or has to change it for any reason, he may lose his concentration and rhythm of the game.

Drago is also known for using the same cue stick for many years and for having certain rituals before each shot.

In addition to these quirks, Drago also believes in the importance of luck in billiards.

He believes that sometimes luck can be more important than skill, and that it is important to be in tune with the table and the balls.

Despite his quirks and superstitions, Tony Drago is a very successful player and has won several major titles in his career, including the European Billiards Championship in 1998 and the World Pool Masters in 2003.

100

Habits and superstitions: Mika Immonen.

He is a professional billiards player from Finland,
who has been one of the most successful
players in the sport's history.

In addition to his skills on the pool table, Immonen is known
for his superstitions and rituals before and during matches.

One of Immonen's most notable superstitions
is his use of blue socks during competitions.

He has stated in several interviews that he wears blue socks
because it's his lucky color, and that he wears
them in every important competition.

He has even said that if he forgets to bring his blue socks
to a tournament, he feels uncomfortable and destabilized.

Another ritual that Immonen follows before every
shot is cleaning his cue with a towel.

He has said that he does it to make sure that the cue is
always clean and slides smoothly through his fingers.

In addition to these superstitions, Immonen is also known
for his focus and concentration on the pool table.

He has described himself as a mentally strong player and has
said that he practices meditation and visualization to help
him stay focused and relaxed during matches.

101

Habits and superstitions: Earl Strickland.

One of Strickland's most well-known
quirks is his obsession with shoes.

He always plays with the same shoes and makes
sure they are clean and in perfect condition.

It is also said that he has several pairs of the same shoes
in his closet in case something happens to one of them.

Another of his superstitions is that he never
steps on the lines of the pool table.

It is said that this is because he believes that
stepping on a line can bring bad luck.

Additionally, Strickland is very particular about the
position and alignment of the balls before starting a game.

If the balls are not perfectly aligned, he will adjust
them until they are exactly where he wants them.

As for his behavior on the pool table, Strickland is known
for his emotional and sometimes explosive playing style.

Over the years, he has had several confrontations
with other players and referees due to his
behavior on the table.

If you have enjoyed the curiosities of billiards presented in this book, we would like to ask you to share a review on Amazon.

Your opinion is very valuable to us and to other billiards enthusiasts who are looking to have fun and learn new knowledge.

We understand that leaving a comment can be a tedious process, but we ask that you take a few minutes of your time to share your thoughts and opinions with us.

Your support is very important to us and it helps us continue creating quality content for fans of this amazing sport.

We appreciate your support and hope you have enjoyed reading our book as much as we enjoyed writing it.

Thank you for sharing your experience with us!

★ ★ ★ ★ ★

Printed in Great Britain
by Amazon